MW00789811

20
Life Lessons
FOR YOUR TWENTIES

Farima Wassel Joya

Copyright © 2016

Printed in the United States

20 Life Lesson Series, Volume 1
20 Life Lessons for your 20s

First Edition

By: Farima Wassel Joya

ISBN-13: 978-0692703915 (7 Treasures Press)
ISBN-10: 0692703918

Published by 7 Treasures Press
www.7treasures.com
7tpress@7treasures.com
(510) 275-3497

10 9 8 7 6 5 4 3 2 1

To my son, Suhrab Joya

Imagine life as a blank canvas; how would you paint yours?

Introduction

Life is an interesting journey. As time passes by, you grow up without noticing anything different from day to day. You have the opportunity to become mature after passing through every obstacle that comes your way. Each obstacle teaches you a unique lesson that only you can experience. For the rest of your life, you will follow your knowledge and wisdom to go through your life journey as an individual. From time to time, you will realize that what you have is not enough, and that is when reading and learning from other people's experiences come in handy. People share their wisdom in the hopes of making a difference in other people's lives. The 20 life lessons included here are humble yet unconventional lessons that will help you make your life a pleasant journey.

Understandably, you have many distractions in your life now that keep you preoccupied with small details and away from looking at the big picture of your life; or, maybe your maturity level is not ripe enough for you to figure out everything that is ahead for you. You are not alone. For a very long time your wants, needs, emotions and finances have been controlled by others – your parents, peers, institutions, government, society and media

– naturally or as a result of other people's greed. This control needs to stop at some point, and you will need to take charge of how you live your life.

If you live a life of ignorance and follow others or let their perception rule you, your life is a lost cause. You are given the gift of one life to live, and it is up to you how you experience it. It really does not matter what anyone thinks of you. The most important point in life is that you live by your own rules and values to be completely satisfied with who you are and what you do.

You are at the beginning of your journey, and these 20 life lessons will help you jumpstart your journey of life filled with your unique gifts to this universe. I only wish that you utilize these lessons and find your own path of life with ease and joy.

SHARING IS CARING

I've shared these 20 life lessons with my son, who is 22. He thinks he knows everything, and honestly, he knows a lot more than I give him credit for. This is true in every parent-child relationship, but the big lesson here is that he understands he has to write his own chapters in life and I am and will always be a stepping stone he can use to jump even higher.

You, too, must understand that whoever shared the gift of this book with you loves you and cares about you. After reading it, please pass it on to someone who you love and care for a lot.

*If money was not an object,
what would you do
with your time?*

1

FORGET TO PLAN FOR THE REST OF YOUR LIFE

At this stage of your life, of course, you can't wait to start and jump into your future. You think you know what you want and what you need to do. Some of you have plans for additional schooling, some want to work, some are very confused as to what to do, and some of you think you know what you need to do. But, I am suggesting that you wait and don't plan who you want to become in the future now. You will need to know yourself better and need to do a lot more real-life learning before you will be ready to decide who you want to become.

Your body has and is still going through many physical changes; things are so different that you don't know what has happened to you and who you are. You look and sound like an adult; you have the energy, guts and are brave enough to take on any challenges. But, inside, you are lost and a bit confused. You need to take this time to know your strengths and weaknesses and widen your imagination and experience to know what kind of rules you want to live by, and how you will choose a path that is solely yours. You are not a productive machine or part of an ignorant herd to be controlled and moved around. You will need to be the driving force of your life.

Although your parents and everyone else expects you to be a productive and contributing member of society right out of high school, you should know better. In order to take control of your life in the future, you will need to take your time to know what really makes you happy and how you really can live the best life that you can live. In that case, you will embrace life with all its pleasures and beauty.

2

MAKE A VISION BOARD

Draw a map of your ideal life as you imagined it during your childhood and adolescence. While you are exploring your options, never lose sight of your childhood imagination, as those beautiful imaginings might be part of your true longings and desires. You'll need them handy and ready to reach when you need to make bigger decisions about your life later on. So have a journal, a photo journal, or a file on cloud to record them all. Record every detail from your past that brought you joy.

You can change your vision board as often as you like. You can add to or take away from it. Your needs, wants, desires and goals change constantly, so your vision board should be a reflection of your desires and wishes.

Have your vision board very clear in mind and enter into your journey, which can be long-term education for a specific career, a long-term trip, vocational training, a volunteer opportunity abroad, or adventures of backpacking or traveling to different cities. During this journey, different types of opportunities will show up in your life and you'll need to choose whether to take them or not. Your vision board will help you make these decisions.

Review your vision board often and memorize it. If there's an opportunity to meet someone that you really want to meet, take it. When an opportunity comes along that you will go on a tour to somewhere on your vision board, take it; when an opportunity for something that you need to experience comes along, sign up for it. You won't regret it at all.

3

GIVE YOUR PARENTS A REASON TO TRUST YOU

Eighteen years is a long time for both your parents and you to get to know each other, but most of the time, parents are so busy with their own lives and making rules for you that they forget to take the time to really know you. On the other hand, you grew up so fast and have surprised your parents with the things you do and how much you have grown up.

Your parents wanted to present a well-behaved, working, good person to society. They worked very hard to raise you with good standards and values that you will carry on after them. However, you will always be their children, and they will always feel they are your savior. It is very natural for parents to say no and to stop you from doing wild things, because naturally they are protecting you. It's their instinct. So let them be, but for your comfort and freedom to part ways with your parents with their love and support without feeling guilty or hurting them in any way, just give them reasons to trust you before you leave them. Save money, organize and clean your room, take the garbage out without asking, help with other chores when you are not expected to, say what's on your mind and why you think that way, introduce your friends to them, and make sure they know that you are involved in good activities with your friends, like playing sports, helping a family member move, or volunteering at a local charity organization.

You will have peace of mind anywhere you are, and your parents will be at ease knowing that you are okay and that you can take care of yourself in any situation.

4

DETACH FROM YOUR OLD FRIENDS AND MAKE NEW ONES

During your childhood and adolescence, your friends are your life. You think you can't live without them. You share everything with your friends, every little secret of your life. Any pleasures that came to your life had something to do with a few good and best friends. However, there is some bad news about that: that feeling and that bond is often only until high school or maybe college. After that, you all develop your own individual personalities and your needs are not the same anymore. This is the time to separate and make new real-life friends. Your skills, talents, strengths and weaknesses are different from those of each one of your friends.

You will have to decide to pursue your goals and dreams according to your own abilities.

You don't have to lose your friends forever. In fact, a loving and supporting friendship is to detach from them physically, so you can be available emotionally to support each other throughout life.

This is also a wonderful time to flourish your connection and friendship with a few good friends that you can trust in good and bad times. You will need to expand your circle and meet more people from different realms of life. You'll need to find the right people to look for inspiration and guidance in different areas of your life. Good friends will always be with you and will never want to harm you in any way. They'll protect you, laugh with you, motivate you and give you good advice.

You'll live longer and happier if you have a circle of good and trusted friends that you can share the deepest issues of your life with and still feel safe. Some of these friends will be friends with you for the rest of your life. So, when there are moments that you feel like no one understands you, your friends, even if they are across the world, will understand you and will listen to you.

5

Develop a unique character trait

Develop your unique trait and character. It should be something that people know you by: loving, caring, polite, respectful, curious, honest, quiet, loud, funny, goofy, etc. You want to develop your personality so people can remember you. You don't need to take life so seriously at this point because you'll have a long time for living a serious life. Now is the time to have fun with one strong point that others can think of and you'll come to mind instantly. You are young, beautiful, charismatic and full of life. Share a good feeling or something good that proudly says something unique about you.

Make yourself known and stand out from the crowd. Be present and participate; surprise people with your hairstyle, fashion choices or activities.

6

TAKE YOUR FINANCES SERIOUSLY

As you are entering the road to independence, managing finances is a new area for you. The financial system is a sophisticated one and really requires financial literacy to be able to stay on top of your finances. The sad part is that schools don't teach you much about financing and the credit system, and what you have learned from your parents might not be enough for you to move on. Now is the time for you to learn the inside out of how the credit system works and learn how it can bring you prosperity or enslave you for a long time.

The credit system is a wonderful system that makes life easier and more efficient if used properly. You can have access to a much bigger amount of cash than you can ever save for yourself. You can use this money to use for anything you need.

The financially smart people use other people's money to invest and make passive income for themselves. The biggest and best use of credit is for buying real estate. However, it is very important to understand the terms and consequences of accessing the unlimited source of cash before using it. Apply for one or two cards to use it for emergencies and to build your credit history. Just remember to pay it off as soon as you can.

You also need to be wary of signing up for large educational loans. Once you are pretty sure of what you want to study, if you sign up for the loan, it is okay. But you should avoid signing up for educational loans if you are not sure about all aspects of the career that you will be having. You'll waste time, energy and money only to find yourself with a career choice that does not make you happy.

For now, if you spend as much as you earn and spend only on your needs, you will be fine.

7

PICK YOUR ROLE MODELS, BUT FOLLOW YOUR HEART

When you were growing up, there was a person or were people that inspired you: you watched them on television, you read their books, you heard them talk. Those are the people that you are naturally drawn to. They have something that you want a piece of. You are inspired; they say one word or one sentence that changes your life forever.

Your role models are human beings just like you. They had goals and dreams and they followed to be where they are, but your strengths and abilities are different from theirs. You are not them. You are your own unique source of creation that has yet to be developed and discovered. Sometimes, following role models becomes obsession, stalking, and a worthless chase that will take you nowhere. Your role models are going on their own path. You need to follow your own path too, getting spurts of energy, motivation and inspiration from them along the way. Make a new destiny for yourself. You deserve it.

People who appear to be tall and stand like a mountain from a distance are like tiny dirt balls piled up together. It is true that nothing seems to be the same when you look at them up close. People are the same; everyone—even our role models, celebrities, sports champions, politicians— is a human being that has good days and bad days. So let them inspire you, but never give up your unique creativity and personality for them or because of them.

8

BE ACTIVE

Try every sport activity you can get your hands on for a hobby or out of curiosity. At this time in your life, it is so important for you to burn energy. You can create and produce the energy of a lifetime in twenty-four hours; too bad that you can't store it for later years of life. Your energy needs to be burned, your muscles need to get oxygenated, your heart needs to pump blood, and your lungs needs to suck the air as hard as possible. Get out and play rough.

Watching sports channels or reality shows on television are not ideal activities for young people. Playing games or spending time on the computer at different social media sites kills creativity as well as healthy cells in your body. Get out and get active, no matter what you do. The important part is that you do something physical – even if it's washing the car or mowing the lawn.

You will need to do some form of exercise for the rest of your life, and how will you know which physical activities you enjoy or you are good at without trying? So never assume that you are good or bad at a specific type of sports if you haven't tried it. And, stay away from the gender stereotypes in sports; it is all a general perception that can be dead wrong. Try it for fun and for the appreciation of the sport itself.

9

PLAN A SOLO TRIP

Before you settle down with a job or a family, plan a solo trip to somewhere new. it is a life-changing opportunity. You will learn how to navigate alone and get what you want. Meeting new people, seeing new areas, learning new languages, and trying new activities will add years of experience to your life. Think of your solo trip as a life boot camp that will prepare you for your future ups and downs in life.

You'll appreciate life, broaden your imagination, adapt to diversity and learn to connect with people beyond interaction within your comfort zone. This experience will set you on a path to take more trips with your family and enjoy the experience.

Being away from familiar people and places will make you stronger and tougher. You will have a chance to rely on your own to maneuver and survive. This will help you later in life to be independent minded which will take you through many tough situations in your close relationships.

10

EXPLORE ART

Music, painting, drawing, writing, cooking and crafts develops your brain and keeps your happiness level at a high.

You might have already explored your artistic talent during your school years and know exactly what is your artistic ability. Try to experience as much as you can and as many disciplines as you can in order to know your passion, your patience and your tolerance for detailed works of art.

Creating art and having a hobby that you like and you are good at will keep you away from negative thoughts and emotions and might be a savior if you go through tough times in life. Art is the best medicine when you are not feeling good physically or emotionally.

If you are really good at creating and using the right side of your brain, you might consider it as a career. If you do something with passion and effortlessly, you will enjoy life more without working a day in your life. Never underestimate your strengths and artistic talent, and never let anyone's opinion change your course for what you'd like to do in life. A five-star chef lives a much happier life than a two-star physician.

11

Don't get emotionally involved

Unless you have found someone that you are feeling true attraction to, you cannot afford to play emotional games with the opposite gender. This is the time for you to explore life and know yourself better. It is very important to know yourself before expecting anything – love, care, affection, time, energy, trust, honesty and commitment – from another person who is at the same level of maturity as you are.

Playing emotional games with people you are friends with or have a connection with is like swimming in dull and dirty water. You waste the energy of the best years of your life trying to find clarity, but you'll never find it. It will drain you and the other person and is a negative energy force on your young life.

When you connect with someone that you feel could be the person you will spend the rest of your life with, your heart and your body will tell you that, but never assume that your physical attraction to that person is love and that you are made for each other. This is a wrong assumption on your part. Take your time, test the waters to get to clarity, and then start swimming with ease.

12

MONITOR YOUR COMMUNITY, YOUR COUNTRY AND THE WORLD

The world is constantly changing from one generation to the next. You need to monitor what is happening in your community, your country and the world. You'll need to see outside of the box of your comfort zone and your familiarity. You might find your million-dollar idea while monitoring what is needed in your community, your country or even the world.

Because you are young and the future belongs to you, you will need to participate in every dialogue that is about your future. You can read the news;

follow your politicians and the developing new laws that will affect your life in the future.

Most of you live in a democratic country and you have the opportunity to choose your leaders and your laws. It is a great loss if you don't participate in the electoral process and stay ignorant of who decides what happens in your life and your future. So participate in every election and use your voting rights to make a better life for yourself and the next generation.

13

Avoid self-destructive behaviors

Legally, you are free to make any decision about your own life. You are free to choose any path you like, but never abuse your freedom to harm yourself and your future in any way by overdoing anything – over-partying, over-drinking, over-sleeping, over-spending, overworking and over-wasting.

From this point on, only you can restrict yourself from your own freedom and choose how you want to spend your time, energy, talent and money. All you need to know right now is that freedom to choose to overdo anything has taken young people in a direction that has made many people lost for many years until they have made the decision to make it right again.

When you have enough confidence on yourself that you can restrict yourself from self-destructive behaviors – whatever they may be, you can hang out in any crowd and dare to take on any challenging activities.

14

Admit you don't know

It is inevitable that you will make mistakes, and making mistakes at this stage of your life can be very valuable for your future. You don't need to know everything or make things up along the way as you go. It is just better and easier for you to admit that you do things based on everything that you know, but if it is wrong, you'll try to do it better the next time.

You are on a journey of life, a journey that everyone lives only once. The amount of information that you need to know to live a perfect life is so vast, it goes beyond the span of your lifetime. So, it's not necessary for you to know everything. You just need to observe your life every day and add to your knowledge every day. Your task is to make life enjoyable for yourself and others around you. Admitting your weaknesses or that you don't know something will get you out of any hard situation and will teach you a lesson that you would not have learned otherwise. Be open and flexible.

15

SAY NO TO PEER/PARENT PRESSURE

Peer pressure is always present during your school years. You are in some sort of unofficial competition and are pressured to do things or be someone that you are not and don't want to be. You want to build a reputation and are willing to go to great lengths to earn or keep your reputation. This means you use your energy and talent to live up to someone else's expectations or standards. Now, you can stop that. Your peers are not you and don't want what you want. They have their goals and ambitions and you have your own.

Your parents might try to pressure you into becoming something that you are not or don't

33

want to be. While respecting their vision of how you will live your life, you need to ask them to take a step back and let you figure it out for yourself. When you know what you want to do or become, ask them for their support; they'll be glad to help you in any way they can. But now is the time to say no, even if it is hard, in order for you to create your own future with your natural talents and strengths.

16

SPEAK YOUR MIND

At your age, you don't have to be correct or say the right thing all the time. Be curious and ask questions. Let people know what you honestly think about issues and give them your reasons in a humble way. However, keep the balance of how much you say, when and where. Only if you can share your mind at the right place with the right people, you can be effective in sending your messages across. Otherwise, you either miss the opportunity to say something or you come across as goofy or arrogant.

You already know that you are on a journey to learn and experience life. This curiosity will speed up your maturity and will help you live a fuller and happier life. And, when you find out that you were wrong or did not say the right thing, simply admit you didn't know as much as you know at the present moment. This will make you an adaptable and humble person, and will help you to grow and become wiser every day.

Most likely, you and your peers place a lot of value on other people's perception of you. This is why some of you are reserved and do not share what's on your mind. Believe in yourself and believe that you have fresh ideas about how things should be or should be done. Voice your opinion, talk louder, ask questions, and never assume that you understand. If something happens and you don't know why, ask and find out the truth about people's behavior. Never assume you know the answer. The more questions you ask, the more you add to your experience and wisdom.

When you are curious and ask questions at the right moment, it means that you live in the moment and you are paying attention to what goes on around you. You are in a journey of life and you have only one round of living it to the fullest with happiness and health. It's your time on earth; this is why you should never hold back or procrastinate – because you might not have the same opportunity again.

17

Trust your guts, take risks

Most likely, your parents raised you in a protective bubble to ensure your safety. Now is the time to get out of that bubble and experience life against other people's expectations. If you have a strong feeling or desire and you know that you can do it, you will accomplish it. Take the risks now, when you are young, because as you get older, you will add layer after layer of responsibility and you will not be able to take risks.

However, you need to prepare and take calculated risks to ensure your success in your adventures. You need to test the grounds, learn the ropes and overcome smaller obstacles before trying to challenge yourself for bigger adventures. For instance, if you want to climb Mount Everest, you need to climb many other mountains before you pack your bags for Everest because it is your responsibility to ensure your safety and success.

18

HELP PEOPLE TO HELP YOU

At this point in your lifespan, you are about to start to reach out to give and receive what you can. Life changes and you change with time. Your needs and wants change from time to time, and you need the help of others to get to where you want to be, but you have to give at the same rate or even higher if you can. You will always have something that someone else does not have. At this point, you have enormous physical energy and the capability to give, so always be on the lookout for opportunities when you can volunteer to help. At the same time, don't be afraid to ask for help, because someone else has an unlimited pile of what you need.

When you are helping and solving a problem for someone, you will need to be fully involved. Go the extra mile because going the extra mile will differentiate you from the rest. You'll stand out as a great friend and a reliable person.

19

FIND YOUR PASSION

You'll have a greater chance of succeeding in life if you can figure out what is your passion. Try to answer this question: "If money was no object, what would you spend your time on?" If you can narrow down your answers, you might find your passion. However, you can have more than one passion at a time; you don't need to choose between them. You just need to combine them if possible. If you are passionate about food and photography, become a food photographer; if you are passionate about fashion and writing, become a fashion writer; if you are passionate about politics and traveling, work for an international political organization.

If you are not sure and need more time to figure out what really makes you happy, remember your childhood. What were the highly happy memories you have in your life? Were you doing better with a specific subject in school? Biology? Chemistry? History? Language? You might find your clues from your past experiences.

Otherwise, pick a subject that interests you – sports, food, entertainment, music, art, history, politics, invention, building, or any global issues – and learn every detail about the subject. If you are still interested in learning more, go for it; that might be the subject you are passionate about.

You live in the information age, or maybe the post-information age. Once, people invested a lot of energy and money to gain knowledge that was not as readily available as it is today. All you need today is the imagination and desire to use the information and put yourself on an enjoyable ride through life's journey. Tomorrow's successful and happy people are the ones who specialize in one thing and go all-in. Become an expert at one thing that interests you and makes you happy.

Once you figure out your passion, strengths and weaknesses, wants and needs, and goals and dreams, then you are ready to make long-term plans of how you will spend your next three, five, and ten years.

20

BE FLEXIBLE & ADAPTABLE

Life is an active journey. Majority of the time, things will not move forward according to your plans and desires. When you are flexible and adapt to any changes that come your way, you will be able to rise above obstacles and find your path. You might go off-path for a short time, but you'll have to know that it is part of your journey. When you have your vision board and your goals are clear, you will find your way back to harmony and ease in life.

The life journey is not a straight line; it has ups and downs. There will be a time that you feel stuck or you don't see the result you are wishing for. You might be at the low dip of your journey. And, there will be times when you feel you are on top of the world; you have everything you wanted; that's when something happens & you are dragged down. You just need to anticipate this shift all the time and be flexible enough to not resist for unnecessary pain or wrong impulse decisions.

The most important lesson of this journey is that you will never be at a standstill point. You are constantly moving – either up or down. When you don't lose your integrity and compassion on the highs, and not lose hope and confidence on the low slopes, you can live your life as a balanced & humble human being in peace and pleasure.

Perhaps this is the most important lesson of all that you will need to know and remember for the rest of your life. So, learn how to be flexible and adaptable to your circumstances at every moment of your life.

Enjoy your exciting – one of a kind - journey on Planet Earth.

ABOUT THE AUTHOR:

Farima Wassel Joya, born and raised in Afghanistan, has gone through many obstacles to be where she is today. She lives in the Hawaiian Islands and enjoys a simple life. She is a multi-passionate author, publisher, and practicing yogi on the path to self-discovery and higher spirituality. Please visit www.7khazana.com for more information.

Made in United States
Cleveland, OH
18 December 2024

12162356R00031